PUFFIN BOOKS

GLORY GLORY

In the *Nou Camp* stadium, Teddy Sheringham's eleven-year-old son, Charlie, sitting in the VIP section and clad in a United shirt with his father's name on the back, noticed that the Barcelona players who had been sitting around him watching the match were beginning to leave. They had seen enough to decide that the result was a foregone conclusion. Returning his attention to the match, Charlie scanned the pitch until he caught sight of the familiar number-ten shirt. If ever he had wanted his dad to score, it was now.

The huge clocks at either end of the stadium clicked up ninety minutes. At the same time, a touchline official brandished an electronic board above his head, indicating that there were three minutes of stoppage time remaining. Time was running out on the Treble.

To Daniel

GLORY GLORY

FERGUS KELLY

PUFFIN BOOKS

PUFFIN BOOKS

Published by the Penguin Group
Penguin Books Ltd, 27 Wrights Lane, London W8 5TZ, England
Penguin Putnam Inc., 375 Hudson Street, New York, New York 10014, USA
Penguin Books Australia Ltd, Ringwood, Victoria, Australia
Penguin Books Canada Ltd, 10 Alcorn Avenue, Toronto, Ontario, Canada M4V 3B2
Penguin Books (NZ) Ltd, Private Bag 102902, NSMC, Auckland, New Zealand

On the World Wide Web at: www.penguin.com

Penguin Books Ltd, Registered Offices: Harmondsworth, Middlesex, England

First published 1999
1 3 5 7 9 10 8 6 4 2

Text copyright © Fergus Kelly, 1999
Photographs copyright © PA Photos
All rights reserved

The moral right of the author has been asserted

Set in Baskerville

Made and printed in England by Clays Ltd, St Ives plc

British Library Cataloguing in Publication Data
A CIP catalogue record for this book is available from the British Library

ISBN 0–141–30734–X

CONTENTS

CHAPTER ONE

NOU CAMP

David Beckham could scarcely believe what he was seeing. Moments earlier, looking up from his position on the pitch, his eye had been caught by a sudden glint of floodlight on polished silver from beyond one of the touchlines. As it flashed once more, Beckham realized that it was the European Cup, in the hands of a UEFA official. As he looked again, he noticed there was something else about the trophy: there were ribbons attached to its handles – in the colours of Bayern Munich.

The representative of European football's governing body wasn't the only person who thought that the swiftly impending outcome of the competition's 1999 Final was more or less beyond doubt. High up in the stands of Barcelona's cavernous *Nou Camp* Stadium, the world's media were already composing their reports for the television bulletins and the following day's newspapers, having reached a similar conclusion, the English journalists among them regretfully noting that this match had proved one hurdle too many in Manchester United's historic quest for the unprecedented Treble of FA Premiership, FA Cup and European Cup.

Bayern Munich had maintained a 1–0 lead since scoring early in the contest, and rarely looked like relinquishing it. To the 91,000 spectators in the magnificent stadium that was lit up like a starship, and to the 200 million television viewers watching from all corners of the planet, it seemed as if a German team would once again confound the dreams of their English opponents, just as their national side had in the 1990 World Cup semi-finals in Italy, and again in Euro '96 at Wembley. And this time it wasn't even going to go to penalties.

United had stepped on to the pitch nearly an hour and a half previously to be greeted by a tumultuous spectacle. The *Nou Camp*'s vast tiers, towering away far above their heads into the gathering dusk, were swathed in red-and-white banners and flags wherever the players looked. Equally breathtaking was the cacophonous wall of sound that hit them almost with the force of a physical blow. The Bayern supporters were dwarfed – both in their numbers and in the noise they generated.

But, virtually from the outset of the match, it was

those Bayern supporters who looked more likely to be celebrating at the final whistle. In only the sixth minute, the Germans were awarded a free kick just outside United's penalty box, after Ronny Johnsen was ruled to have brought down Bayern's formidably built forward, Carsten Jancker.

Shortly before midfielder Mario Basler shaped to strike the free kick, his team mate, defender Markus Babbel (whom United had once been interested in signing), joined the end of the defensive wall. In what was evidently a well-rehearsed set-piece, Basler curled the ball around the corner of the wall at which Babbel was standing. Peter Schmeichel did not the see the ball until far too late, and the giant Danish goalkeeper remained rooted to the spot as it sped into the bottom left-hand corner of his net.

While the goal was obviously unwelcome, it did not represent a disaster. After all, United had fallen behind on a number of other momentous occasions during the season. On this evening, however, United were not at their best. Certainly, they took the play to Bayern for prolonged periods of the match. But the dazzling interchanges of passes at high speed, which had been the hallmark of United's success during their progress to the brink of the Treble, were a rarity. Promising moves broke down too often in the final third of the pitch and, despite having the majority of the possession, United fashioned few clear-cut chances from it.

For that, much of the credit went to the Germans' defence. Superbly organized by veteran captain, thirty-eight-year-old Lothar Matthäus, it frustrated United's forwards at every turn. Despite having scored fifty-three goals between them throughout the season, Dwight Yorke and Andy Cole were never allowed the time or space to develop potential scoring situations. Bayern's Ghanaian-born defender, Samuel Kuffour, in particular, was a marker that Yorke could never shake off, always tackling and harrying.

From his seat on the touchline, Bayern's coach, Ottmar Hitzfeld, watched and savoured his team's display. Hitzfeld was an old adversary of United manager, Alex Ferguson. Two years previously, he had been in charge of another German club, Borussia Dortmund, and had triumphed in this same competition – after defeating United 1–0 both home and away in the semi-final.

As the final progressed, there was a growing sense of unease, both among United's fans in the stadium and those watching at home, and between the various pundits commentating on the match for TV and radio, that Fergie had committed a tactical blunder which was in danger of gifting the European Cup once more to Hitzfeld.

In selecting his team for the final, Ferguson had been deprived of both his club captain, Roy Keane, and Paul Scholes, who were both suspended after receiving yellow cards in the semi-final. The absence

4

of each was bound to be strongly felt: Keane because of his driving runs and fierce tackling in midfield, Scholes for his goal-poaching instincts.

Ferguson had sought to overcome their omission by switching David Beckham to Keane's central midfield role, playing Ryan Giggs on the right wing, and bringing in Swedish international Jesper Blomqvist on the left flank. But it quickly became apparent that this was a flawed formation.

Beckham, while performing tirelessly in the middle of the pitch, was badly missed in his more customary role on the right wing, where his pinpoint crosses had contributed so much to United's all-conquering season. As a natural left-winger, Giggs was playing out of position. Blomqvist, meanwhile, was having a nightmare against the uncompromising Bayern defence. Starved of the crosses from Giggs and Beckham upon which they normally thrived, Yorke and Cole consequently struggled to make an impact up front.

Acknowledging this problem, Ferguson substituted Teddy Sheringham for Blomqvist in the sixty-sixth minute. Almost immediately the reorganized United looked more threatening. But instead it was Bayern who came closest to scoring, twelve minutes later. Mehmet Scholl, himself a substitute who had come on minutes earlier, chipped the ball over Schmeichel, only to see it bounce off the post and into the arms of the grateful goalkeeper. A second goal then would surely have finished off United.

With ten minutes remaining, Ferguson made his next move. Ole Gunnar Solskjaer was introduced in place of Andy Cole. But once again, it was Bayern who nearly put the final beyond doubt. In the eighty-fourth minute, Jancker, with his back to goal, hurled himself at the ball with a ferocious overhead kick. It smashed against the crossbar, and rebounded to safety.

Around the stadium, United's fans urged their team to redouble its efforts to find that elusive equalizer in the dying minutes. In pubs and homes throughout Britain, watches were anxiously consulted. At her parents' home in Hertfordshire, Victoria Adams of the Spice Girls began to reconcile herself to the fact that maybe this was one trophy which her fiancé, David Beckham, would not win.

On the tiny Caribbean island of Tobago it was late afternoon, and in the front room of Grace Yorke's home, twenty friends and relatives crowded round the colour television set bought for her by her son, Dwight, and tried to will the ball into the back of Bayern's net from thousands of miles away.

Meanwhile, back in the *Nou Camp* stadium, Teddy Sheringham's eleven-year-old son, Charlie, sitting in the VIP section and clad in a United shirt with his father's name on the back, noticed that the Barcelona players who had been sitting around him watching the match were beginning to leave. They had seen enough to decide that the result was a foregone conclusion. Returning his attention to the match, Charlie scanned the pitch until he caught sight of the familiar number-ten shirt. If ever he had wanted his dad to score, it was now.

The huge clocks at either end of the stadium clicked up ninety minutes. At the same time, a touchline official brandished an electronic board above his head, indicating that there were three minutes of stoppage time remaining. Time was running out on the Treble.

CHAPTER TWO

THE BUSBY BABES

The beginning of the dream which culminated that night in the *Nou Camp* Stadium can be traced back to the wreckage of a bomb-shattered Old Trafford, more than half a century previously. Surveying the rubble where the stands had once stood and the crater in the pitch, one day shortly after the end of the Second World War, stood Manchester United's new manager. He was a Company Sergeant Major physical-training instructor who had served throughout the war's six-year duration, and his name was Matt Busby.

Busby, a Scot, was only six when his father, a miner, was killed in the First World War, and he had been brought up by his mother, who herself worked at the pithead of a coal mine. During his playing career, for Manchester City – with whom he collected an FA

Cup winner's medal in 1934 – and Liverpool, he had been regarded before the war as a stylish and creative midfielder.

After winning the FA Cup in 1909 and the League Championship in 1911, United (originally known as Newton Heath when formed in 1878) had fallen into decline between the two World Wars, and City had been Manchester's premier team. Busby immediately set out to change that.

One of his first acts upon becoming manager was to appoint Jimmy Murphy as his coach. He had befriended Welsh-born Murphy in Italy, where they had both served during the war. More importantly, Murphy possessed an unrivalled ability for spotting talented youngsters and moulding them into brilliant players.

Busby and Murphy began with very few resources at their disposal. For the first four years after the war United did not even have a ground, and Busby's office was situated in a £30 Nissen hut. The club played their home games at rivals' Manchester City's Maine Road until Old Trafford re-opened in 1949.

Even so, they soon constructed what would be the first of three great Manchester United teams during the Busby era. In 1948, the club won the FA Cup for only the second time in its history, thanks to stars including captain Johnny Carey, winger Charlie Mitten and striker Jack Rowley, winning 4–2 against Blackpool whose line-up included the legendary Stanley Matthews.

A year later, Tottenham Hotspur tried to lure Busby away from United, offering him what was then the considerable sum of fifty pounds per week to become their manager. Who knows what might have happened if he had accepted the offer? Fortunately for United, he didn't, and in 1952 they won the League Championship for the first time in forty-one years.

Even at the height of this early success, however, Busby was already looking ahead. Aided by Murphy's genius, he developed a scouting network that stretched across Britain and ensured that United were nearly always first in the race to sign the most impressive schoolboy players.

Bobby Charlton, for instance, travelled to Old Trafford, aged fifteen, from his home in the north-east, when he had been expected to join his local team, Newcastle United. 'The buildings were black and there was fog everywhere and I wondered if I'd made the right decision,' he remembered years afterwards. 'But I soon changed my mind when I arrived at Old Trafford and Jimmy Murphy said I would love playing here because they had the most wonderful players. Manchester was a gruesome place then, but nevertheless the players lit up the scene.'

Youngsters like Charlton were nurtured through the youth team ranks and, as soon as they were considered mature enough to cope, promoted to the first team. In one of many close parallels with Busby's methods, it was a scheme which Alex Ferguson would later revive to great effect.

Very soon, the youngsters had taken over the first team. The media christened them the 'Busby Babes', and hailed them as the most exciting side in English football. They were also the most successful, winning the League Championship in 1956 and 1957 – narrowly missing out on what would have been the century's first Double, when they lost the FA Cup Final to Aston Villa.

Busby would later recall: 'I felt I was in a position where I could have sat back for ten years while the team played. It was that good. I used to go to grounds hoping that the other team would score an early goal to start us off and get us playing at our best.'

Despite the Championship triumphs, it would be a mistake to imagine that the lifestyle of those young United players bore even the faintest resemblance to that enjoyed by their counterparts today. Bobby Charlton worked in an engineering firm during the week for the early part of his United career, while, in his first three seasons at the club, defender Bill Foulkes combined his football with working down a coal mine in nearby St Helens. It paid him more too – fifteen pounds per week, compared to his eleven-pound weekly wages at United.

Busby's other great innovation at this time was to introduce United to European football. Very few English clubs took part in international competition, for the Football League viewed it as an unnecessary addition to the demands of the domestic game. But, in 1956, Busby leapt at the opportunity presented when United were invited, as English champions, to take part in a new competition which had been created by a French sports newspaper: the European Cup.

After winning through the early stages, which included an amazing 10–0 rout of the Belgian champions Anderlecht in the first round, the competition eventually brought United up against the team then acknowledged to be the finest in Europe: Real Madrid of Spain. The two sides met in the competition's semi-final, and United lost 5–3 on aggregate. But valuable lessons had been learned from the experience, and Busby looked forward to going one step further in the following season's competition.

That season was 1957–8, and by then the Busby Babes were truly in their pomp. Up front, Tommy Taylor and Dennis Violett terrorized defences; in midfield Eddie Colman danced round opponents before they knew what had happened; and there was no faster or more skilful right-winger than Johnny Berry. Few opposing teams could breach a defence which included Roger Byrne, Bill Foulkes and Jackie Blanchflower. And then there was Duncan Edwards.

Even in this team of stars, Edwards stood out. He could play anywhere: central defence, midfield, or attack. He made his debut for England aged only eighteen – which was then virtually unheard of – and by 1958, when he was still a mere twenty-one, he was already regarded as the most promising player English football had ever produced.

Among those who flocked to watch Edwards was a fifteen-year-old schoolboy called Terry Venables. Despite being a Tottenham Hotspur fan, Venables pestered his father Fred to go with him to Spurs' arch-rivals Arsenal, to see Edwards and United in a League game.

He was not let down. United won a thrilling confrontation 5–4 and Edwards opened the scoring after only ten minutes with a twenty-five-yard drive of awesome power. 'That was my moment,' said Venables, years later. 'We had travelled in to see him and, with the latecomers still arriving, he had me turning to my dad with a "Did you see that?" look.' Venables added: 'He was a great tackler, he was a good passer, he scored goals, and he was a rock in defence. He was left-footed, but he could use the right too. It was exciting to look at him and think how good he was going to be.'

He would never find out. What the young Venables could not know was that he would be one of the last people to see Edwards in action. Four days after that match, Edwards and seven of the other Busby Babes perished in the Munich air disaster.

On 6 February 1958, British European Airways Flight 609 had landed in the German city of Munich to refuel on the way back to Britain from Yugoslavia, where United had drawn 3–3 with Red Star Belgrade, to go through on aggregate to the European Cup semi-final.

The runway at Munich was treacherous, covered in snow and slush. Two attempts to take off were aborted. Only ten minutes after disembarking from the aircraft following the second failure, United's squad of seventeen players, accompanied by club officials and journalists, were shepherded back on board. Once more the airliner gathered speed. But this time it overshot the end of the runway, crossed a road, and careered into a house. The impact tore the tail off, and the remaining fuselage smashed into a tree and then collided with a petrol tanker, which exploded.

Roger Byrne, Geoff Bent, Eddie Colman, Mark Jones, David Pegg, Tommy Taylor, Liam Whelan and Duncan Edwards were killed. Edwards clung on to life for fifteen days after the disaster, and a stunned nation prayed he would pull through, but in vain.

Three members of United's backroom staff also died, along with eight British journalists, two crew, and two other passengers – a total of twenty-three. For weeks afterwards, it was feared that Matt Busby would join that toll. He suffered severe injuries in the crash, and at one point had the last rites administered to him by a Catholic priest.

His assistant, Jimmy Murphy, was not on the trip,

because by this time he was also manager of Wales, and had been involved that night in a World Cup qualifier in Cardiff.

With Busby hovering between life and death, Murphy found himself temporarily in charge of a team whose biggest stars had all been wiped out in an instant. It seemed as if Busby and Murphy's dream of making Manchester United the greatest club in Europe had died with them.

CHAPTER THREE

KINGS OF EUROPE

For two weeks, Matt Busby lay in an oxygen tent in a Munich hospital, unaware of the scale of the disaster that had befallen his team. Doctors feared that if he learned how many of his team he had lost, it could destroy his will to live. But one day, during one of his infrequent bouts of consciousness, he overheard a clergyman in the corridor outside his room, saying: 'Duncan Edwards is dead.' Busby demanded to be told the truth.

It fell to his wife, Jean, to break the news. Busby went through his players name by name, and whenever he mentioned one who had been killed in the crash she simply shook her head. The manager blamed himself for taking the team into Europe in the first place, and only his wife talked him out of quitting the game. Slowly the injured, including Busby, recovered, although Johnny Berry and Jackie Blanchflower never played again. Three months after the tragedy, Busby limped into Wembley on crutches for the FA Cup Final.

Amazingly, under the guidance of Jimmy Murphy, United had reached the Final. But their depleted team was defeated 2–0 by Bolton Wanderers. In the European Cup semi-final – which United had reached on the night of the Munich air disaster – they also went out, despite a 2–1 win at Old Trafford in the first leg, beaten 4–0 in the return leg in Milan.

After possessing a team that he had been convinced was on the brink of greatness in European competition, Busby now faced having to build a new Manchester United almost from scratch. With the faithful Murphy once more at his side, Busby again resolved that the future lay in cultivating the talent of young players.

The most precocious of all those talents was a fifteen-year-old who arrived in Manchester from his home city of Belfast in 1961. George Best was instantly identified as a player of phenomenal potential, already able to do things with a football that seasoned professionals at the club would not even attempt.

He was swiftly offered an apprenticeship but, in an early example of the changing moods which would later bring a premature end to his career, a homesick Best returned to Belfast after only a week. He was eventually persuaded back and made his League debut at the age of seventeen in 1963. A new United legend was born.

Other promising youngsters like Nobby Stiles came through the ranks, while Bobby Charlton, who before Munich had been on the verge of the first team, blossomed into one of England's top strikers. Busby also brought out the cheque book to strengthen his new team, and among those he signed in 1962 was a Scottish forward called Denis Law from Italian club Torino, for what was then a British record transfer fee of £115,000. Law, a wonderfully acrobatic player, was renowned for his fierce shooting from mid-air and his heading ability.

In 1963, United won their first trophy since the Munich disaster, defeating Leicester City in the FA Cup Final. Then, in 1965, they won the League Championship, a feat they repeated in 1967 – the fifth title of Busby's reign. It was clear that he now possessed his third and perhaps greatest Manchester United team. However, the European Cup still eluded him.

United had been denied in the semi-final of the competition for the third time in 1966, a 1–0 victory in the second leg at Old Trafford against Partizan Belgrade not being enough to overturn a 2–0 defeat in the first leg. It was a bitter end to a season that had promised so much, especially after United had gone to former European champions, Benfica of Portugal, in an earlier round and scored a scintillating 5–1 win – masterminded by one of the finest performances of Best's career.

Still only nineteen, Best conjured up two early goals, as United ran riot against a side who had previously never lost at home in the European Cup. The admiring Portuguese fans christened Best 'El Beatle' – a fitting title for the first footballer to command the same adulation as a pop star.

In response to the disappointing semi-final defeat by Partizan, Busby merely pursued his European dream with even greater vigour. By the start of the 1967–8 season, he had reinforced his team still further with the signing of goalkeeper Alex Stepney from Chelsea, and more skilful youngsters were knocking on the door of the first team, including an eighteen-year-old called Brian Kidd.

After coming through the early rounds, United eventually found themselves in the semi-finals pitted against Real Madrid, who had previously won the European Cup five times. In a closely contested first leg at Old Trafford, United just edged the match, winning 1–0 with a goal from Best. But it looked a slender lead to take to the enormous Bernabeu Stadium in Madrid, in front of a baying crowd of 120,000 Spaniards.

By half-time in that second leg, it looked a lost cause. United trooped dejectedly into the dressing room 3–1 down with Real in total control. Busby was waiting for them. 'Look, we're losing,' he said. 'But it's still only 3–2 on aggregate. If we're going to go down, let's go down making a fight of it! We might as well lose 6–2 as 3–2!' Similarly stirring half-time words from Alex Ferguson would be a vital factor in Manchester United's European Cup win, thirty-one years later.

It was certainly a transformed United who came out for the second half of the tie against Real. Attacking relentlessly, they were finally rewarded, eighteen minutes from the end, when Best headed on a Paddy Crerand free-kick, and David Sadler forced the ball home.

Then, five minutes later, the goal that put United into their first European Cup Final came from a very unlikely source. Best was again the provider, going past a defender to cross into the penalty area. Who should race on to the end of the cross but veteran defender Bill Foulkes, the only survivor of the Munich disaster (apart from Bobby Charlton) to be still playing for United. He scored, and United were through.

The 1968 Final was staged at Wembley on 29 May, and United's opponents were Benfica. Their team included the brilliant Eusebio, the star of Portugal's run to the World Cup semi-finals two years previously, where they had only narrowly been beaten by England. United, meanwhile, were without the injured Denis Law.

A scoreless first half was notable chiefly for Eusebio

hitting the bar and for the number of fouls committed on Best. Eight minutes into the second half, United scored. From a cross by Sadler, Bobby Charlton rose at the near post and looped a header over the Benfica goalkeeper. It was a lead that did not last.

In the final fifteen minutes, United noticeably flagged, and Benfica began to seize the initiative. In the seventy-ninth minute, a cross was headed down into the path of midfielder Graca, and he shot past Stepney. As the ninety minutes ticked away, Eusebio suddenly burst through the United defence in the final seconds. Only Stepney stood between him and what would have been certain defeat for United. Had Eusebio placed the ball, he would probably have scored. But instead he elected to blast it, and Stepney hurled himself to his left to fingertip the ball to safety.

That miss seemed to knock the wind out of Benfica's sails. It was they who now looked weary, and United took full advantage. In the first minute of extra time, Best received a pass in midfield, swerved past one defender, and then danced round the Benfica goalkeeper before swivelling to poke the ball into the net.

Within minutes, Brian Kidd, celebrating his nineteenth birthday that day, headed home from a Charlton cross, and then repaid the compliment, setting up Charlton to crash in the fourth goal. As the final whistle blew, an exhausted Charlton sank to the turf and wept. Maybe he was remembering his team-mates whose lives had ended so abruptly on that frozen runway at Munich.

Matt Busby was certainly thinking of them as he watched Charlton hoist the European Cup above his head moments later. 'The moment when Bobby took the Cup, it cleansed me,' he said. 'It eased the pain of the guilt of going into Europe. It was my justification.'

CHAPTER FOUR

END OF AN ERA

The 1968 European Cup triumph represented the greatest moment in Manchester United's history to that date. But this pinnacle of achievement also signalled the beginning of a decline in the club's fortunes.

Matt Busby, who was knighted shortly after the victory over Benfica, announced his retirement as manager only six months later. He had been in charge at Old Trafford for twenty-three years, and by finally winning the European Cup had achieved his lifetime ambition. He was not to leave United, however. Instead he would move upstairs to become general manager. The search for a successor began.

Many big names were mooted, but the eventual choice was Wilf McGuinness. His appointment as Sir Matt's replacement made him the youngest manager in the First Division at thirty-one. With hindsight, that was a mistake. McGuinness, a former player who had joined the training staff after his career was cut short by injury, lacked the authority to deal with some of United's older stars.

The second problem was Sir Matt himself. Instead of making a clean break with the past, his continued presence cast a long shadow over the new manager. In McGuinness's only full season in charge, in 1968–9, United finished a disappointing eleventh in the First Division. Their defence of the European Cup looked rather more promising, until they came up against AC Milan in the semi-finals, and lost 2–1 on aggregate.

Halfway through the 1970–71 season, McGuinness lost his job. United were teetering on the brink of the relegation zone. Long-established stars like Nobby Stiles, Pat Crerand and Denis Law were approaching the end of their United careers, and their replacements were not of the same calibre. And then there was George Best.

United's failure to win more silverware in the aftermath of the European Cup began to fuel an increasing disenchantment in the temperamental Best. There were still flashes of genius, not least the extraordinary six goals he put past a hapless Northampton Town of the Fourth Division, in the FA Cup fifth round. On that unforgettable afternoon in 1970, United ran out eventual winners by 8–2.

But such displays of artistry were starting to be

outweighed by rather less savoury outbursts of dissent and petulance. He was banned for a month for scuffling with a referee, then was sent off for throwing mud at another one during a Northern Ireland international. He began to skip training, and he missed the team train to a number of League matches.

In exasperation, Sir Matt (who had briefly returned to the manager's seat, to steer United to First Division safety after McGuinness went back to training the reserves) suspended Best for two weeks after he went absent for four days without telling the club. The punishment worked – briefly. The worst, however, was still to come.

In the meantime, United had appointed Frank O'Farrell as their new manager, with Sir Matt moving on to the board of directors. O'Farrell had recently overseen Leicester City's promotion to the First Division, and was generally regarded as an up-and-coming man. Now he had to prove himself in the toughest job of all.

The task proved beyond O'Farrell. Within eighteen months he, too, had departed. Under him, United finished eighth in the League and reached the FA Cup quarter-finals – and for such a demanding club that was not good enough.

O'Farrell's reign was also marred by the continuing problems surrounding George Best. The disappearing acts started again, and he was finally put on the transfer list. The final straw for United's directors was a 5–0 thrashing in the League at Crystal Palace. O'Farrell was fired three days later, and at the same time Best was also told to leave. Unknown to the club, he had already written a letter that day announcing he would no longer play for United.

Into the midst of this chaos came Tommy Docherty. The manager of Scotland's national team at the time, the brash and extrovert Doc was exactly the sort of boss that United's fans craved – someone dedicated to playing attractive, attacking football.

In his first season, Docherty just managed to keep United in the First Division. He also began the long-overdue process of bringing in youthful new talent to Old Trafford, including forward Lou Macari from Celtic.

Out went Denis Law, on a free transfer to Manchester City – a fateful move, as it would turn out – and, in April 1973, Bobby Charlton made his 751st and final appearance in a United shirt. His retirement at the end of a career which included World Cup, European Cup, League Championship and FA Cup winning medals, broke the final link with the Busby era.

The following season, 1973–4, was the worst in United's post-war history. By Christmas they had won only four games and were already flirting with relegation. After nine months away, George Best had ended his self-imposed retirement and offered himself to United's cause. Docherty was wary, and rightly so.

After only twelve appearances, Best predictably failed to turn up for training. He would never play for United again.

The self-destruction of probably the greatest talent the game of football has ever produced (with the exception of Pele) was a true tragedy. He would play again intermittently, for Fulham, for non-league Dunstable Town, and also for teams in the United States. But these appearances served only to highlight how Best's erratic lifestyle had finally caught up with him. Defenders who once would never have got within yards of him now dispossessed him, and the magical pace and ball control, while never totally deserting him, were displayed only in spasms. A bewitching and unique player had been lost to the game.

Whether or not Best's continued presence could have saved United from the relegation that loomed ever larger was doubtful, however. By early February 1974, they were bottom of the First Division. By Saturday 27 April, when Manchester City came to Old Trafford, United had to win to stand any chance of staying up.

The score stood at 0–0 with eight minutes to go, when the ball ran loose in the penalty box. It rolled invitingly to Denis Law – the hero of so many United triumphs – and he backheeled it into the net. There was no celebration by Law as he turned away. Instead his face said it all: an expression of stunned sadness at the enormity of what he had just done.

It was the final ball that Denis Law ever kicked, for he retired immediately after the match, and it condemned Manchester United. Only six years after winning the European Cup, they were now a Second Division club.

CHAPTER FIVE

THE JOURNEY BACK

A new Manchester United arose from the ashes of the disastrous previous season. Tommy Docherty completed the clear-out of the remaining players from the Best–Law–Charlton era. In their place came a new generation of thrilling young stars.

Battling midfielder Sammy McIlroy and the commanding defender and club captain, Martin Buchan, had arrived during Frank O'Farrell's brief period as manager. They were joined by Stuart Pearson, a strapping striker, and, on the wings, by Steve Coppell and Gordon Hill, both of whom possessed electrifying turns of pace.

There was little doubt from very early on in the 1974–5 season that United were returning straight back to the First Division. They played with a style and verve largely absent from Old Trafford since the golden days of the 'Sixties.

Crowds of a size not seen before or since in what was then the Second Division followed them wherever they went. The Old Trafford fixture against United's nearest rivals, Sunderland, drew a phenomenal 60,585 attendance. Clubs that United visited saw their average gates doubled, even tripled. United finished the season as champions with games to spare.

They began their comeback in the First Division at the same breakneck pace. By April, a League and Cup double even looked feasible. But, in the final weeks of the season, they faltered and, in a conclusion which was to be repeated many times in the seasons to come, Liverpool won the title.

United were in the FA Cup Final, however, and the opposition, Southampton of the Second Division, were given no chance. But the underdogs made a mockery of the odds. They stifled United's forward line, and gradually took control of the game. With eight minutes left, a long, crossfield ball found Southampton's little left-winger, Bobby Stokes, in acres of space, and his shot went beyond Alex Stepney.

Docherty and his dejected players vowed to return to Wembley the following season, and were as good as their word. Their opponents this time were Liverpool, who were on the brink of what was then an unprecedented treble. They had already clinched the

League Championship, and were due to meet Borussia Moenchengladbach four days later in the European Cup Final.

Three goals in a five-minute period at the start of the second half settled the 1977 FA Cup Final – and United got two of them. A Stuart Pearson shot and a bizarre deflection off Jimmy Greenhoff gave United their first trophy since the 1968 European Cup, and denied Liverpool a treble which no English club would come near again. Until 1999, that is.

Yet within weeks of delivering his first trophy at United, Docherty was gone. He was sacked after it was revealed that he was having a relationship with the wife of the club's physiotherapist.

The task of continuing the rebuilding of United, which the Doc had successfully begun, fell to Dave Sexton. He was as unassuming as his predecessor was flamboyant. That, and his failure to land any trophies during his four-year stint as manager, meant that he never really endeared himself to United's fans. Sexton's ultimate failure was not for want of money. United spent what were then huge sums on star names, such as Joe Jordan for £350,000 and Gordon McQueen for £495,000, both from Leeds United.

Later, Ray Wilkins was signed from Chelsea for £825,000, and Sexton eventually became the first United manager to breach the £1 million barrier, when he paid £1,250,000 for striker Garry Birtles from Nottingham Forest. Poor Birtles, who had been a prolific scorer under Brian Clough at Forest, seemed overawed by the size of the fee paid for him, and never lived up to it.

The closest Sexton came to success was in the 1979 FA Cup Final, which featured one of the most gripping climaxes even in that competition's history. United were facing Arsenal, and were 2–0 down by half-time. With only four minutes left on the clock, McQueen prodded the ball home in a penalty area mix-up. Then, two minutes later, Sammy McIlroy set off on a mazy run past Arsenal's vainly lunging defenders, before levelling the score. Pandemonium broke out among United's supporters, as extra time beckoned.

But, from the restart, Arsenal went straight back up the pitch, with Liam Brady evading numerous challenges before finding Graham Rix out on the right wing. He crossed, and Alan Sunderland shot past goalkeeper Gary Bailey's despairing hands. This time United could not come back.

In the 1979–80 season, United also narrowly missed out on the League Championship, denied by – who else? – Liverpool, by a two-point margin. But the following year, United could manage only eighth place, despite winning their final seven games in a row, and Sexton was given the sack.

The new manager, Ron Atkinson, was committed

to the sort of open, entertaining football that United's fans have always expected. His first major buy was Frank Stapleton, the Arsenal forward, for £900,000. But that fee paled into insignificance next to the one Atkinson forked out to break the British transfer record, to sign Bryan Robson from West Bromwich Albion. The man who would become known as Manchester United's and England's 'Captain Marvel' cost £1.5 million. It was an enormous sum, but Atkinson claimed at the time: 'Bryan is the best midfield player in the country.'

Atkinson would be proved absolutely correct, but few people who saw Robson arrive at West Brom as a fifteen-year-old schoolboy would have believed him, as he was only five feet two inches high, and weighed just over seven stone. Once he made the first team at West Brom, he then broke his leg twice in successive seasons. But Robson overcame these deficiencies with the sheer hard work and determination which would soon become apparent to United's fans.

A respectable third place in the First Division at the end of Atkinson's first season did nothing to compensate for the fact that Liverpool won the title again, and the positions were exactly same again in 1982–3.

In the FA Cup and League Cup, however, United were heading to Wembley on both fronts in 1983. The League Cup had by now been renamed the Milk Cup, after the competition's sponsors, the Milk Marketing

Board, and when United did eventually reach the final, their path was barred again by Liverpool.

After only twelve minutes, United were ahead, thanks to the youngest player ever to score in a Wembley final. Norman Whiteside, aged seventeen, had already made history as the youngest player to appear in a World Cup, for Northern Ireland in Spain the previous summer – a record previously held by Pele.

But his goal did not prove enough, and Liverpool fought back to win 2–1. United now pinned their hopes on the FA Cup Final.

Their opponents were Brighton, who had already been relegated from the First Division that season. But they were not to be under-estimated, as United knew better than anyone since that 1976 shock defeat by Southampton. A 2–2 draw was followed by a replay, also at Wembley, and Whiteside broke yet another record, becoming the youngest player to score in an FA Cup Final, in a 4–0 landslide.

In Atkinson's time as manager, United never finished lower than fourth in the First Division. They won the FA Cup, defeating Everton 1–0, in 1985 thanks to another goal from Whiteside, and the previous year enjoyed an exciting run to the European Cup-Winners' Cup semi-finals, beating Barcelona (including a certain Diego Maradona) along the way, before narrowly going out to Juventus.

More top-class names, like Gordon Strachan from

Aberdeen, Danish international Jesper Olsen, and Ipswich striker Alan Brazil, were signed. A highly promising forward, who had come from the same youth team as Whiteside and who was called Mark Hughes, emerged.

But if it wasn't Liverpool depriving United of the coveted League Championship, it was their Merseyside neighbours, Everton. What turned out to be Atkinson's last opportunity to land the title came in the 1985–6 season, and United could not have made a better start.

They won their first ten League matches on the trot, and by early November 1985 were ten points clear at the top of the table. But, yet again, United stumbled, and let that precious lead slip through their fingers. The club finished fourth, and fans were even less pleased when Mark Hughes – who had quickly become a firm favourite – was sold to Barcelona for £2 million.

The writing was on the wall for Atkinson when United lost their opening three matches in the 1986–7 season. By November 1986, they were fourth from bottom. A 4–1 defeat by Southampton in the Littlewoods Cup (the latest version of the League Cup) sealed his fate. He was sacked on the morning of 6 November and, on the same afternoon, United's chairman, Martin Edwards, was on a jet travelling to Scotland to meet the new manager. His name: Alex Ferguson.

CHAPTER SIX

FERGIE

An incident early in Alex Ferguson's managerial career illustrated the sort of man that Manchester United were getting as their new boss. He was in charge of Scottish First Division team, St Mirren, at the time, and had become increasingly irritated by what he regarded as the apathy shown towards the club by the population of its home town of Paisley. Which was why, one day, the inhabitants of the town's housing estates heard a commotion outside and peered through their windows to discover that the noise was coming from a loudspeaker rigged up on top of the car belonging to the manager of their local football team; he was urging them to get out and watch his players in their next match.

This passion and fiercely competitive spirit was

later to become apparent to the players of Aberdeen, the club which Ferguson moved to next. They knew only too well that Ferguson's desire to win spilled over into everything he did – even a game of Trivial Pursuit. Some of them were even convinced that the boss, a obsessive fan of this and other quiz games, was not averse to peeking at a few of the answers beforehand, so determined was he not to lose.

There was never any doubt that Ferguson would accept the challenge of taking on the hottest seat in football when Martin Edwards came calling. For here was a stage to match even his relentless ambition. By the end of the same day on which Ron Atkinson was sacked, Alex Ferguson was installed as his successor.

Alexander Chapman Ferguson was born during the Second World War in Govan, home of the city of Glasgow's then flourishing shipbuilding industry. His father worked in the shipyards on the Clyde (Fergie's home in Cheshire is called Fairfields, after the yard in which his father was based), and it was a trade into which the young Ferguson initially followed him, working as an apprentice toolmaker.

Even then, the combative side of his nature soon came to the fore, when he led an apprentices' strike in the factory in which he worked. But Ferguson had already set his sights on a career in football. His father did not approve at first. When Ferguson came home one Saturday after a match, to announce that he had scored a hat-trick that day, the response was: 'Go back and get a proper job.'

In his playing days, Ferguson was a bustling forward, but he did not exactly set the world alight. He was also hardened early on to the pain of rejection. While playing for Dunfermline Athletic, he was informed only forty-five minutes before the kick-off of the 1965 Scottish Cup Final against Celtic that he had been dropped. It was an experience he never forgot.

Going into management after his retirement as a player, Ferguson guided St Mirren to the Scottish First Division title, before leaving to take over at Aberdeen. There, he quickly presided over the most successful period in that club's history.

At the time of his appointment, Scottish football was dominated by its two biggest clubs, Celtic and Rangers of Glasgow, who were known together as the 'Old Firm'. Between them, they had won the last fifteen Scottish championships. What Ferguson proceeded to do was to break the Old Firm's stranglehold. Under him, Aberdeen won three Scottish Premier League titles, four Scottish Cups and one Scottish League Cup.

But the high point was undoubtedly a May night in Gothenburg, Sweden, in 1983, when Aberdeen defeated the mighty Real Madrid 2–1 to lift the European Cup-Winners' Cup. It was a magnificent achievement by the young team that Ferguson had created, and it also alerted a lot of clubs south of the border to his ability. In the early 'Eighties, both Arsenal and Tottenham Hotspur made approaches to Ferguson when their managers' jobs fell vacant. But there was only one post that he really wanted.

At his first press conference at Old Trafford, he said: 'It is incredible to think that a club of United's size have not won the League Championship in twenty years. That is a great challenge to me.' Of his time at Aberdeen, he added: 'I had a lot of success and very little failure. It's up to me to maintain that momentum with United. I have a much bigger stage and base here.'

On taking over from Atkinson, Ferguson guided United away from the lower reaches of the First Division to finish eventually in eleventh place – United's lowest end of season position since they were relegated in 1973–4. It was eight months before he ventured into the transfer market, signing full-back Viv Anderson from Arsenal, and paying £850,000 for Celtic striker Brian McClair, who had amassed thirty-five goals in his final season in Scotland. They were soon followed by central defender Steve Bruce, who came from Norwich City, also for £850,000.

McClair swiftly established that he was good value for his fee, becoming the first United forward since George Best, two decades previously, to score twenty League goals in a season. Sadly, that was the only bright spot in the 1987–8 season. After starting positively, United fell away once more and, though they recovered enough towards the end of the season to finish runners-up, it was the same old story above them: Liverpool were champions.

Ferguson opened his cheque book again. Mark Hughes, a huge crowd favourite at Old Trafford, came back from Barcelona for £1.5 million. He had reluctantly departed to the Spanish club two years previously, and was teamed up front with Gary Lineker by Barcelona's coach, Terry Venables. But Hughes never really settled in Spain, and he was delighted to return. Ferguson also went back to his old club, Aberdeen, to sign Scottish international goalkeeper Jim Leighton, for £750,000.

His other main task was to concentrate on building up the youth team. In a throwback to the days of Sir Matt Busby, United under Ferguson once more scoured the country for the best young players, and among the earliest recruits was a seventeen-year-old from Torquay United called Lee Sharpe.

The results, however, did not improve. United finished a disappointing eleventh in 1988–9, and their season was effectively over as early as March when they went out to Nottingham Forest in the FA Cup sixth round. Attendances at Old Trafford were the lowest in twenty-two years.

Yet more big names were bought – England midfielder Neil Webb from Nottingham Forest for

£1.5 million, defender Mike Phelan from Norwich for £750,000, and Danny Wallace from Southampton for £1.5 million.

Two of Ferguson's most significant signings arrived at around this time. Paul Ince, much sought after by a number of clubs, joined from West Ham United for £2 million, and the British transfer record was broken to bring defender Gary Pallister from Middlesbrough for £2.3 million.

And still things got worse. The murmurs of dissatisfaction with Ferguson, which had begun the previous season both in the media and among supporters, were becoming much more strident. The most popular joke doing the rounds, referring to the vast sums that the manager had spent in the transfer market, was: 'Why isn't the Old Trafford pitch more healthy-looking when Fergie's put £13 million of manure on it?'

A 5–1 thrashing by rivals Manchester City in September 1989 led to the first calls for Ferguson's head; by Christmas of that year, United were struggling in the lower half of the table, and fears were even being expressed about relegation.

It seems scarcely feasible now, but in December 1989 the sports pages of the *Daily Mail* carried an article headlined: 'United fans agree – "Fergie has to go".' Supporters were quoted as saying that after three years in charge, Ferguson had been given enough time, and that he should make way for Bryan Robson to take over as player-manager. Another newspaper called Ferguson 'Manchester United's least successful manager in modern times', and referred to Old Trafford as 'the house of broken dreams'.

At the end of the first week of January 1990, United travelled to Nottingham Forest in the third round of the FA Cup. It was their last chance to salvage something from a dismal season. If United lost, there seemed little doubt that the same thing would happen to Ferguson's job.

Sir Matt Busby trains with his legendary 'Busby Babes'.

United's George Best and teammate David Sadler celebrate winning the 1968 European Cup against Benfica.

Alex Ferguson, the manager who brought the success of the 1990s.

Eric Cantona, the United legend, playing in a Munich memorial match.

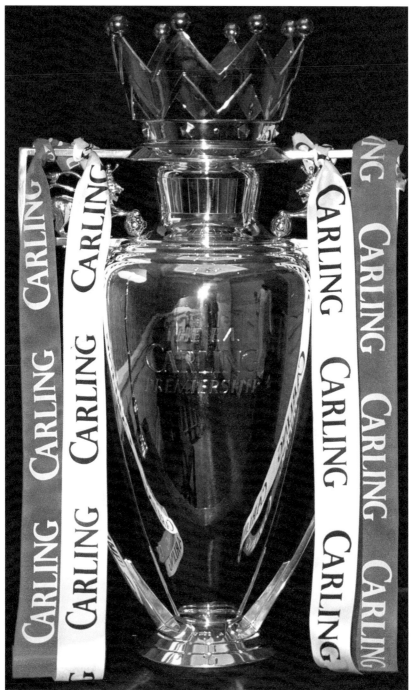

The Carling Premiership trophy of 1999 – destined for Old Trafford.

Paul Scholes celebrates his decisive goal in the FA Cup final.

United celebrate part two of the treble.

David Beckham tackles Bayern's Markus Babbel early in the Champions League final.

Moments of glory … for Peter Schmeichel …

… and the whole United team as the treble is won.

David Beckham – simply the best.

CHAPTER SEVEN

CHAMPIONS AT LAST

Manchester United's extraordinary haul of championships and cups throughout the 'Nineties can be traced back to a cold but bright January afternoon in 1990 at the City Ground, Nottingham, and a young forward called Mark Robins. His goal, the only one that day in the game against Nottingham Forest in the third round of the FA Cup, not only kept alive United's season, it also probably rescued Alex Ferguson from the sack.

To be fair to Martin Edwards and the United board, at no time did they suggest that Ferguson's job was in danger. While success was slow in coming on the pitch, they were impressed by the way in which the manager had completely overhauled the club's scouting and youth coaching systems.

Equally significantly, Brian Kidd was about to be promoted to be Ferguson's assistant manager. Kidd, a nineteen-year-old European Cup winner back in 1968, was a logical appointment. He had previously been Youth Development Officer at Old Trafford, in charge of eleven-, twelve- and thirteen-year-olds coming to the club. Those youngsters were soon to become more important to United than Kidd, or anyone else, could predict.

Mark Robins was already a product of United's youth policy, and so too was Lee Martin. After a difficult campaign, which included a nail-biting semi-final against Oldham Athletic, United found themselves at Wembley for the 1990 FA Cup Final, and it was Martin, a twenty-year-old full-back who was not a regular first-team choice, who blasted the winner in a midweek replay against Crystal Palace, following a 3–3 draw the previous Saturday. At last, United had won something. Ferguson declared: 'This is the greatest day of my life.' There were many more to come.

Just as importantly, his collection of expensive signings was starting to gel. While consistency in the League continued to elude them, United became a formidable cup team. In 1991 they reached the Rumbelow's Cup Final, but after doing all the hard work in the earlier rounds, defeating Leeds United, Liverpool, and Arsenal – by an amazing 6–2 scoreline at Highbury, which included a hat-trick by Lee Sharpe – they lost 1–0 at Wembley to Sheffield Wednesday.

United were to have better fortune in the European Cup-Winners' Cup. A relatively smooth passage through the competition eventually brought them up against Barcelona in the final, in Rotterdam, Holland. For Mark Hughes, it was a reunion with the club which had discarded him, and he had something to prove.

For virtually the entire ninety minutes United outplayed their illustrious Spanish opponents, and Hughes in particular was outstanding, scoring both goals in a 2–1 win. It was United's first European success since 1968, and it came in the first season in which English clubs had been allowed back into European competition since the Heysel Stadium disaster six years earlier.

Ferguson continued to strengthen the team. Full-back Denis Irwin was bought from Oldham, and flying winger Andrei Kanchelskis came from Donetsk in his home country of Ukraine. One position that the manager felt was still vulnerable in the United line-up was in goal. To remedy that situation, he travelled to Brondby in Denmark, to sign that club's giant international goalkeeper, Peter Schmeichel, in 1991, for a fee of £550,000. It represented probably the best business in the transfer market that Ferguson ever transacted.

For much of its duration, the 1991–2 season looked like being the one in which United would finally cast off the millstone of not having won the

Championship for a quarter of a century. Schmeichel did not concede a goal in his first four matches, Bruce and Pallister looked impregnable in central defence, Robson, Ince and Webb ran the show in midfield, and on the flanks United were at their most deadly, thanks to Kanchelskis, and a precocious young Welshman who, even though just seventeen, was already being compared to George Best: Ryan Giggs.

By the time United reached the Rumbelow's Cup Final for the second successive year, with only a month of the season remaining they were top of the First Division, with only Leeds United anywhere near them. United beat Nottingham Forest 1–0 with a McClair goal to win their third trophy in a row. But the fixture list was piling up – at one stage they played four matches in six days – and Leeds whittled away and then overtook United's lead.

A fortnight after their Wembley triumph, United had missed out on the Championship again, losing 2–0 at Liverpool, while Leeds were winning 3–2 against Sheffield United. It was a devastating blow. Ferguson said: 'Maybe this is the final lesson for us, the ultimate experience in humility and a reminder to our younger players of how it feels to lose.'

In the summer of 1992, the existing First Division clubs broke away from the Football League to form the new FA Premiership, but in the opening months of the 1992–3 season, United looked no more likely to win the new League than they had the old one.

Then came a turning point. In November 1992, chairman Martin Edwards received a telephone call from his counterpart at Leeds United, Bill Fotherby, inquiring whether Denis Irwin might be for sale. Edwards told Fotherby he was wasting his time. Meanwhile, Ferguson, who was sitting in Edwards's office at the time, whispered: 'Ask about Cantona.' In a matter of days, the Frenchman had signed for £1.1 million.

Eric Cantona's signing was seen as a risk. He came with a reputation for trouble, principally dating back to his early career in France, after incidents which included throwing the ball at a referee's head, and then calling a disciplinary committee 'idiots'. After being banned, he announced his retirement at twenty-five.

English football came to his rescue. Following a brief spell at Sheffield Wednesday, Cantona swiftly emerged as a star at Leeds United, and he played an important role in helping them deprive United of the Championship the previous season.

Now he provided the final link in Ferguson's all-conquering team. Not only did Cantona have a habit of popping up to score vital goals, he invariably provided the final, telling pass for others to score. As George Best said admiringly, not long after Cantona's arrival: 'He has given this team a brain.'

Aston Villa stood between United and the new Premiership title, running them neck and neck, until

Wednesday 21 April 1993. That evening, Villa finally cracked, losing 3–0 at Blackburn Rovers, while United won 2–0 at Crystal Palace, Cantona laying on both goals for Hughes and Ince. With only two games remaining, United were four points ahead. But they didn't need to finish the job. Villa did it for them, losing 1–0 at home to Oldham. United couldn't be caught. The twenty-six-year wait was over.

CHAPTER EIGHT

THE DOUBLES

The day after Aston Villa blew their last chance of winning the 1992–3 Premiership title, Manchester United celebrated their triumph in front of an ecstatic, flag-waving full house at Old Trafford. Watching them defeat Blackburn Rovers 3–1 from his usual seat in the stand, sat a smiling Sir Matt Busby.

It was the moment he had waited more than a quarter of a century to see. It also confirmed to Sir Matt, although he had never really been in any doubt, that in his fellow Scot, Alex Ferguson, United had found his worthy successor, a man who demanded of his teams that they play to the same attacking and adventurous principles.

Eight months later, on 20 January 1994, Sir Matt died, aged eighty-four. Thousands turned Old Trafford into a shrine, laying scarves and other tributes beneath the clock memorial to the Munich disaster which had so nearly claimed his life. One of the messages that was left read: 'You planted the seeds that have made Manchester United the greatest team in the world. Rest in peace, Sir Matt, you have left us in safe hands.'

United, meanwhile, were on the brink of achieving a feat that not even Sir Matt had ever managed. They had begun the season where they left off, in irresistible form. The front line of Cantona, Giggs, Kanchelskis and Hughes swept all before them, and Ferguson had broken the British transfer record yet again the previous summer, to add fearsome tackler Roy Keane to the midfield, in a £3.75 million deal with Nottingham Forest.

The only blot on the landscape was United's short-lived return to the European Cup. They were knocked out in the second round by the much under-estimated Galatasaray of Turkey, who held United 3–3 at Old Trafford, and then, amid controversial scenes including a sending-off for Cantona, 0–0 in the return leg, to go through.

But in the Premiership, United were an astounding fourteen points ahead of their nearest rivals by the start of December 1993, with everyone saying the title race was over even before the New Year. Not only that, but they were also progressing towards the FA Cup and Coca-Cola Cup Finals. An unprecedented treble was on the cards.

Aston Villa put paid to that dream, defeating United 3–1 in the Coca-Cola Cup Final. Then things began to go wrong elsewhere. Cantona was sent off twice in quick succession, and was banned from crucial matches. Blackburn Rovers, managed by Kenny Dalglish, and boasting a very in-form Alan Shearer up front, were narrowing the gap in the Premiership.

Shearer scored twice to beat United 2–0 in their Premiership clash at Blackburn, and cut the deficit between the two clubs to only three points. Eight days later, United were 1–0 down with forty seconds of extra time to go in their FA Cup semi-final against Oldham Athletic. From being poised to win three trophies, United were in danger at that moment of ending with nothing. Mark Hughes' last-gasp equalizer, crashed home on the volley as the referee checked his watch, was the turning point in United's season.

They thrashed Oldham 4–1 in the replay, and in the Premiership the pressure finally told on Blackburn, who lost crucial matches and handed United their second successive title. Chelsea stood between United and the League and Cup Double – a feat that then had been achieved only three times previously in the twentieth century, by Tottenham Hotspur in 1961, Arsenal in 1971, and Liverpool in 1986.

United added their own name to that illustrious list,

thanks chiefly to Eric Cantona, whose two penalties put them on their way to a 4–0 victory. Before he stepped up to take the first one, Chelsea's Dennis Wise bet Cantona £100 that he would miss. The Frenchman did not betray a hint of nerves or doubt, to send the goalkeeper the wrong way. Wise paid up after the match.

The FA Cup Final also signalled the end of Bryan Robson's glorious United career – and not in the circumstances he might have hoped for. In the week leading up to the Final, Ferguson informed his former captain that he would only be on the substitutes' bench. Telling Robson was a task made even more difficult for the manager because he remembered vividly the pain he had felt after being left out of the 1965 Scottish Cup Final.

After the triumph of the Double, United set out the following season with the European Cup their number one priority. Drawn in a group with IFK Gothenburg of Sweden, Barcelona, and their conquerors from the previous year, Galatasaray, they began brightly.

Gothenburg were beaten at Old Trafford 4–2, and a creditable 0–0 draw was wrested from the difficult trip to Turkey. Next came home and away ties against Barcelona. The Old Trafford leg ended 2–2, with a cheeky Lee Sharpe back-heel saving United from defeat.

In the return at the *Nou Camp* Stadium, United

were tormented as Barcelona, with a team which included names like Romario, Stoichkov, Hagi and Koeman, went on the rampage and ran out 4–0 winners. It was the beginning of the end. Another defeat, 3–1 by Gothenburg in Sweden, sealed United's fate. A 2–0 win at home to Galatasaray could not save them. United were out again.

At least in the Premiership they went into the new year of 1995 two points behind leaders Blackburn. United had also signed the high-scoring Andy Cole from Newcastle United, for £7 million. The prospect of him playing alongside Cantona was a mouth-watering one for the Old Trafford faithful.

It was a partnership, however, that was over before it had hardly begun. Three days after Cole's debut, United travelled to Crystal Palace in January 1995. It was the night that Eric Cantona lost his head – and almost his career – when he launched a flying kick at a spectator who had taunted him. The headline in the following day's *Manchester Evening News* seemed to sum up the situation: 'Ooh-Aah – He's Gone Too Far.'

United immediately banned the Frenchman for the rest of the season, which meant he would miss their final seventeen games. The Football Association imposed an even longer ban until a month into the start of the next season. And, finally, a magistrate jailed him for two weeks for common assault. The sentence was later quashed, and Cantona was ordered instead to perform 120 hours of community service.

He carried out the sentence working with young footballers at United's training ground, The Cliff.

Even without Cantona's influence, United kept pace with Premiership leaders Blackburn until the final Sunday of the season. They needed to win at West Ham, and hope that Blackburn would lose at Liverpool. Blackburn did lose, but United could only draw, with Cole being blamed for missing numerous chances.

United were forced to relinquish the other half of their Double at Wembley, when they were defeated by a single goal by Everton in the FA Cup Final. It was the first time in six years that United had ended a season without a trophy.

Everyone waited to see how Cantona would cope on his return to the Premiership, on Saturday 1 October 1995, at home to Liverpool. Many football commentators believed that he was a marked man, who would be provoked by rival fans and opponents alike into exploding again.

Running on to the pitch to the strains of the theme from *The Magnificent Seven* – which was his shirt number – it was as if Cantona had never been away. Within sixty-eight seconds of starting, he had set up a goal for Nicky Butt. Then, with twenty minutes remaining, and United by now 2–1 down, Giggs was brought down in the penalty area. Cantona picked up the ball without a second thought, placed it on the spot, and scored.

Before Cantona's return, United had started the season slightly shakily, and many observers were quick to point to the summer sales of Paul Ince to Inter Milan, Mark Hughes to Chelsea, and Andrei Kanchelskis to Everton. In their place, Ferguson had promoted youngsters. They included the Neville brothers, Gary and Phil, in defence, Nicky Butt and David Beckham in midfield, and Paul Scholes, who filled Cantona's position in the Frenchman's absence.

A comprehensive 3–1 defeat on the opening day of the season at Aston Villa had prompted former Liverpool player Alan Hansen to claim memorably on BBC1's *Match of the Day*: 'You don't win anything with kids.' An early exit from the UEFA Cup at the hands of little-known Russian club, Rotor Volgograd, seemed to vindicate Hansen. In the Premiership, meanwhile, Newcastle United, managed by Kevin Keegan, had raced twelve points clear by January 1996.

It was the cue for an incredible United fightback. Both in the Premiership and in the FA Cup, they were unbeatable, and Cantona was their inspiration. One of his most crucial goals came in the top-of-the-table clash at Newcastle, which United won 1–0. The Geordie team lost their nerve in vital games, and United, with the experience of two Premiership triumphs already behind them, came through to clinch the title for a third time. A 3–0 win at

Middlesbrough – managed by Bryan Robson – made sure.

United had also reached their third FA Cup Final in a row, to face Liverpool. Four minutes from the end, it was, inevitably, Cantona who scored the winner. United had won their second Double in three years – something no other club had ever done.

CHAPTER NINE

AU REVOIR, ERIC

I t was a truly remarkable goal, the sort of goal that will be talked about for as long as people follow Manchester United. On the opening day of the 1996–7 season, United began the defence of their Double at Wimbledon. They were already 2–0 up when the ball broke free, just inside the United half, and came into the possession of David Beckham.

He decided in a split second what he was going to do. That was all the time it took for Beckham to look up and spot Wimbledon goalkeeper Neil Sullivan off his line. The United midfielder was still standing just behind the halfway line when he launched his extraordinary shot. Those watching who thought it was merely a speculative effort suddenly realized that the ball's trajectory was taking it straight into the roof of the Wimbledon net. So did Sullivan, but too late to prevent it with his flailing leap.

The goal, greeted by a collective gasp from millions of TV viewers who saw it later that night, symbolized the arrival of perhaps the most promising and richly talented new generation of United youngsters since the Busby Babes. After being introduced the previous season, Beckham, Nicky Butt, Paul Scholes and Gary Neville, all of whom were only twenty-one, were now regulars. In comparison, Ryan Giggs, still a mere twenty-two, seemed a veteran.

Their mentor, United's assistant manager Brian Kidd, who had watched Beckham sign as a fourteen-year-old schoolboy, and who had first spotted Scholes in a children's five-a-side competition, was delighted by the youngsters' progress. 'The attitude of the young players has never been a problem, and won't be. We keep reminding them that work has got them where they are, and that if they stop there's always somebody else ready to come in,' he explained.

United had been busy in the transfer market over the summer. A striker called Ole Gunnar Solskjaer had come from Norway, while his countryman, defender Ronny Johnsen, was signed from a Turkish club. After nearly ten years of magnificent service to United, however, Steve Bruce had departed for Birmingham City – his captain's armband passing to Eric Cantona. Lee Sharpe had also left, joining Leeds United.

One player who was not coming was Alan Shearer. After starring in England's run to the semi-finals of Euro '96 that summer, the Blackburn forward was the target of Europe's top clubs. Alex Ferguson was said to have bid more than £10 million for him. But Shearer was eventually persuaded to sign for his home-town team, Newcastle United, by manager Kevin Keegan, for a then world record fee of £15 million.

Ironically Shearer's debut for his new club was against Manchester United. The two clubs met in the FA Charity Shield, and the Reds cruised to a 4–0 victory. Shearer and Newcastle would get their revenge. After a solid start to the 1996–7 season, United suffered two crushing defeats in a row, and the Magpies administered the first. They smashed five past United without reply at St James's Park.

Barely had United recovered their wits before they were travelling in their next League game to Southampton – not particularly noted for their goalscoring exploits. However, United had always found The Dell a bit of a bogey ground for them, and so it proved with a vengeance. United lost 6–3 and, to cap a miserable day, had Roy Keane sent off. But if they thought that was the end of their troubles, United's shell-shocked players had reckoned without the visit of Turkish champions, Fenerbahce.

The match was their fourth tie in what had now become known as the UEFA Champions' League. United had opened their campaign against group favourites Juventus, narrowly losing 1–0 in Turin. But that was followed by two excellent wins. United defeated Rapid Vienna 2–0 with goals from Beckham and Solskjaer. Then, in their first match against Fenerbahce, in Istanbul, United were even more impressive.

Despite a very hostile atmosphere – which included continuous orders from the public address system for the local fans to cheer on the Turkish team until UEFA officials stepped in to stop it – United came away with another 2–0 win, as Beckham and Cantona scored. That made United's home game against Fenerbahce all the more baffling. The Turks won 1–0, to end United's forty-year record of never having lost at Old Trafford in European competitions.

When Juventus then came to Old Trafford and did exactly the same thing, United's hopes of continuing in Europe were in the balance. They had to go to Rapid Vienna and win, and rely on Juventus defeating Fenerbahce. A stunning save from Schmeichel in Vienna, flinging himself to the ground to scoop out a downward header which looked a certain goal, saved United from falling behind. Then Giggs and Cantona eventually got the goals needed. Juventus also came up trumps, beating Fenerbahce 2–0. United were through to the quarter-finals.

Back in England, United took the Premiership by the scruff of the neck over Christmas. In seven days, they beat Sunderland, Nottingham Forest and Leeds, scoring ten goals in the three matches and conceding none. Among the goal-scorers was Solskjaer, who had swiftly become a huge favourite of the fans. The son of a professional wrestler back in Norway, he was nicknamed the 'Baby-Faced Assassin' at Old Trafford. By the end of January, United were on top of the Premiership again. But Wimbledon knocked them out in the FA Cup fourth round – revenge perhaps for that Beckham goal on the opening day of the season.

In the quarter-finals of the Champions' League, United were drawn against FC Porto, and in the first leg produced one of their finest European performances ever, demolishing the Portuguese champions 4–0, with goals from May, Cantona, Giggs and Cole. A 0–0 draw in the second leg put them in the last four. People started making comparisons with 1968. This was the furthest United had got in the competition since then.

On 9 April 1997, they travelled to Germany to face Borussia Dortmund. Only forty-five minutes before the kick-off Peter Schmeichel was declared unfit, and so Dutch reserve goalkeeper Raimond van der Gouw was drafted in for only his fourth first-team game for United.

Van der Gouw did his job magnificently, until a cruel deflection off Gary Pallister from a shot by Tretschok finally beat him.

Dortmund killed the semi-final in only the seventh minute of the Old Trafford return, with a twenty-yard shot by Lars Ricken in almost their first attack. United queued up to lay siege to Dortmund's goal, but did not take their chances.

United's only consolation was that the previous weekend they had taken a giant leap towards winning the Premiership. At the time, they were two points ahead of Liverpool at the top of the table, so when the two clubs met at Anfield the match was viewed as a virtual decider for the title. Liverpool had a nightmare. Two inswinging corners from Beckham were both met by Pallister, who was given free headers on each occasion; and the final score was 3–1 after goalkeeper David James completely missed a cross, for Cole to nod home.

As in previous seasons, United did not actually win the Premiership on the pitch. A defeat for Liverpool and a draw for Newcastle United, their closest challengers, on the same night, meant that neither could catch United. Before the start of their final game of the season, against West Ham at Old Trafford, Eric Cantona brandished the Premiership trophy, the fourth time United had won it in five years. It would also be the Frenchman's last appearance, as he surprised everyone by retiring at the end of the season.

The legacy that Cantona left behind him was priceless. Ryan Giggs said later: 'He was a winner the day he arrived and now all the players at United have inherited that quality from him. We have all grown up to be winners and he showed us the way. Eric fixed that example in all our minds. We are now a very good side, but Eric set it all up. Over the last few years we've lost key players, but Eric was probably the best of them all.'

The other invaluable gift that Cantona taught was the importance of keeping possession and patiently seeking an opening, especially in European competition. Team-mates recall a training session in which Cantona was encouraging them to play five-yard passes to each other repeatedly. 'What's the point of this? We're in the same position as we were before,' complained one colleague after a while. 'Ah, yes,' replied Cantona, 'but the defenders aren't.'

While United would for ever be in the debt of the departing Frenchman, it was his countrymen, in the shape of Monaco and Arsenal's manager Arsene Wenger, who would confound United the following season. The Reds started the 1997–8 season as if they were taking up where they left off, going nine games without defeat. Up front, Teddy Sheringham had been signed from Tottenham Hotspur for £3.5 million as a replacement for Cantona. On his debut he returned to his old club, and missed a penalty. But he quickly slotted in next to Andy Cole.

Cole, meanwhile, was at last fully justifying Alex Ferguson's faith in him. A growing number of doubters were wondering whether or not the striker would ever fulfil his potential, and alongside Cantona he had not always looked comfortable. But, in one electric burst, Cole smashed eight goals in three games, in the space of only eleven days. First came a hat-trick in a 7–1 rout of Barnsley, then two more in another utterly one-sided win – 6–1 against Sheffield Wednesday, and, finally, there was another hat-trick against Dutch side Feyenoord in the UEFA Champions' League.

United could not have made a better start in Europe. Firstly, the Hungarians of Kosice were swept aside 3–0 on their own ground, and then United tamed the might of Juventus 3–2 on a compelling night at Old Trafford. Behind in the first twenty seconds to Del Piero, United poured forward. Sheringham equalized with a header, Scholes danced around the goalkeeper to give them the lead, and then a Giggs piledriver put the result beyond doubt, despite a late goal from Zinedine Zidane.

Feyenoord, who were later to fall to that Cole hat-trick, were also beaten in the two clubs' first meeting at Old Trafford, 2–1, and United completed the double over Kosice, again by 3–0. By the time they met Juventus in the return in Turin, United were already through to the quarter-finals. Juventus had to win to stay in the competition, and just managed it through a Filippo Inzaghi goal, only eleven minutes from time.

A 0–0 draw in Monte Carlo against Monaco in the quarter-final's first leg seemed to have set up United for a place in the last four. But there was a shock in store. Just as in the previous season, when Dortmund had caught United with an early goal, so this time Monaco stunned Old Trafford into silence, when young striker David Trezeguet lashed the ball past reserve keeper Raimond van der Gouw after five minutes of the return leg. Solskjaer equalized shortly after half-time, but United could not find a winner. It was the climax of a dismal week which was effectively to kill off United's hopes of winning anything that season.

Four days before Monaco ended their interest in the European Cup, United had lost 1–0 at home to Arsenal. The Marc Overmars goal that settled the match that March afternoon was seen by many as deciding the ultimate destination of the Premiership trophy, as Arsenal went ahead in the race. Yet at Christmas, three months previously, that had scarcely seemed feasible. By then United were twelve points clear, and bookies had stopped taking bets on them winning the Premiership again.

There had been warning signs: a terrible injury to United's Roy Keane in only the second month of the season at Leeds ruled him out for the rest of it. It was a critical blow, and United never quite overcame being deprived of his inspirational captaincy. Arsenal had also fired a warning shot across their bows at their first League meeting of the season at Highbury, snatching a 3–2 win. Even so, losing such a huge lead at the top of the Premiership was traumatic.

United won five of their last seven Premiership matches, but to no avail. Arsenal were the champions and, to compound the injury, they also equalled United's record of winning two League and Cup Doubles, by beating Newcastle United 2–1 in the FA Cup Final. The Gunners had established themselves as genuine rivals to United's superiority in English football. Alex Ferguson had once remarked: 'I think losing is a good experience. It reminds you of how hard it was to get where you are.' So how would his players respond to this setback?

CHAPTER TEN

TREBLE CHANCE

On the opening day of the previous season, David Beckham had stolen the headlines with a stunning goal. His name was also on the lips of everyone at the start of the 1998–9 season – but for entirely different reasons. One rash moment in that summer's World Cup in France had transformed Beckham overnight into the most vilified man in the country. With England's second-round tie against Argentina on a knife edge at 2–2, he had been felled by a crude tackle by opposing midfielder Diego Simeone. As he lay, face down, on the floor, Beckham brought his leg up and clipped Simeone.

The Argentinian over-reacted shamefully, collapsing in a heap as if he had just been shot. But Beckham had committed his foolish retaliation right under the nose of the Danish referee, who had no hesitation in sending him off.

The rest of the story has passed into history. Reduced to ten men, England fought a valiant rearguard action and hung on until the penalty shoot-out, in which they sorely missed Beckham's deadball ability, and crashed out of the tournament. So heated was the initial strength of feeling against Beckham that, on his return home, serious doubts were expressed that he would ever be able to play in this country again. Others offered their support. One vicar put a sign on his church noticeboard which read: 'God forgives David Beckham.'

The public debate over Beckham's future went even as high as Prime Minister Tony Blair, who said: 'I should think that no one feels worse about it than David Beckham does. He is obviously going to have to learn from that.' At his lowest moment, Beckham's greatest support came from Alex Ferguson. In a heart-to-heart talk, the United manager encouraged him to weather the storm.

So, instead of hiding away, Beckham lined up for United's opening fixture at home to Leicester City – the most eagerly awaited return since Eric Cantona came back from his nine-month ban for his assault on a spectator. With ninety minutes gone, United were losing 2–1 to Leicester when they won a free-kick. Beckham stepped forward to take it. From twenty-five yards out, he sent a stunning shot round the goalkeeper to save United a point. He had answered his critics in the best way possible.

A week later, United paraded their record signing, Dwight Yorke. The Trinidad-born striker had cost £12.6 million from Aston Villa, and he completed a staggering spending spree by Ferguson. At the end of the previous season, he had bought Dutch international central defender Jaap Stam for £10.75 million from Feyenoord. Despite Holland's passage to the World Cup semi-finals, the general opinion was that Stam had not been particularly outstanding, and some claimed he would struggle to cope with opponents who possessed real pace.

Swedish international winger Jesper Blomqvist had also been signed from Italian club Parma for £4.5 million. The other new face in the United line-up was someone who had been at the club for five years, but whose absence over nearly all of the last season through injury had been a significant factor in the club's failure to win any trophies: Roy Keane.

Yorke was an instant hit, scoring twice on his home debut and filling United with confidence for their first group game in the UEFA Champions' League, at home to Barcelona. The 3–3 draw with the Spanish club at Old Trafford was the curtain-raiser to a host of truly enthralling Wednesday nights in Europe for United. Within twenty-five minutes, Giggs and Scholes put them into a 2–0 lead, but Barcelona clawed back to 2–2. Another stunning goal from

Beckham seemed to have edged the match, but a penalty gave Barcelona the draw.

Three days after that result, United were stopped in their tracks in the Premiership. Arsenal beat them emphatically, 3–0, at Highbury, and Ferguson conceded afterwards: 'We were second best in every challenge.' Arsenal were starting to look like a jinx team for United, having won all of the two clubs' four previous meetings.

In their Champions' League group, United were next up against Bayern Munich in Germany. For the first, but certainly not the last, time that season, the two teams proved that they were very evenly matched, but only a blunder by Schmeichel in the final minute allowed Bayern to snatch a 2–2 draw.

United then put eleven goals in two games past Brondby of Denmark (from whom they had signed Schmeichel), before coming up against Barcelona again. Another thrilling 3–3 draw ensued, United going a goal behind in the first minute, only to go 2–1 and then 3–2 up in a see-saw clash. Brazilian international Rivaldo came to Barcelona's rescue with two goals, one a spectacular overhead kick. A 1–1 draw with Bayern at Old Trafford put both sides through to the quarter-finals, where United learned that they would meet Inter Milan of Italy.

Back home, Aston Villa and Chelsea were the early pace-makers in the Premiership. Just before Christmas, United were beaten 3–2 at home by

Middlesbrough, which kept them in third place. It would turn out to be their last defeat of the season, but at the time the omens did not look good. The following month they were on the verge of going out of the FA Cup.

Facing old rivals Liverpool in the fourth round, United went behind to a goal by Michael Owen after three minutes. With eighty-eight minutes gone, they were still 1–0 down, despite laying siege to Liverpool's goal. Then they won a free-kick. Beckham floated the ball across the goalmouth, Andy Cole headed it down, and Yorke stabbed it home.

A replay loomed. Suddenly Scholes took a pass from Giggs and laid it into the path of Ole Gunnar Solskjaer. Seconds later, the Norwegian was wheeling away in triumph, mobbed by his team-mates, with the ball in the back of the net. Surely United – or Solskjaer – would never be able to provide that type of finish again . . .

Soon after 1999 dawned, United launched a goal blitz which would take them to the top of the Premiership. They warmed up by smashing four past West Ham, then scored six against Leicester, and, in a glorious display of attacking football, thrashed a hapless Nottingham Forest 8–1. Solskjaer came on as substitute, ten minutes from the end – and scored four times. And he still couldn't command a regular first-team place! At around this time, Tottenham Hotspur expressed an interest in signing Solskjaer.

United fans could scarcely guess how grateful they would eventually be that he chose to stay at Old Trafford.

With ten wins from the last eleven Premiership games under their belt, United entertained Inter Milan in the Champions' League quarter-final. After only six minutes they got a dream start. Beckham, who played an inspired game throughout, whipped over one of his deadliest crosses, and Yorke, free of his markers, headed United into the lead. Just before half-time, an almost carbon-copy move – with Beckham once more setting up a Yorke header – put United two up.

In the second half, United squandered further chances, but then required Schmeichel to keep their precious lead. Confronted by a goalbound header from an unmarked Zamorano, the keeper spread himself wide and stunned the Italians by hooking the ball away with his hand. In the final minutes, Schmeichel did it again – parrying a shot from Ventola, and then sticking out a leg to deflect a second effort from the same player.

In the second leg in the San Siro Stadium, Schmeichel once more pulled off a series of breathtaking saves to deny Inter. Even though the Italians finally did go ahead in the second half, Paul Scholes equalized in the dying minutes to guarantee United's semi-final place. The victory was especially sweet for David Beckham, for Inter's line-up included

Diego Simeone, the man responsible for his World Cup downfall.

Having knocked out one Italian club, United now had to face another in the last four, their old rivals Juventus. A brilliant last-gasp equalizer by Ryan Giggs in injury time kept United's hopes alive in the first leg at Old Trafford, after Juventus had taken a first-half lead.

In the space of a week, United were then involved in two of the most pulsating cliffhangers, in even their history. First they faced Arsenal in an FA Cup semi-final replay, following a 0–0 draw in the first match.

After seventeen minutes, Beckham fired a wickedly curling drive beyond David Seaman to put United ahead. Despite Roy Keane being sent off, and Nicolas Anelka having a goal disallowed, United hung on until the sixty-ninth minute, when a shot from Dennis Bergkamp deflected off Stam and pulled Arsenal level.

Then, in the last minute, Arsenal were awarded a penalty. The Treble, which people had only just started talking about as a possibility for United, looked to be dead and buried, especially as it was Bergkamp who was taking the spot-kick. In these situations he hardly ever missed. Bergkamp's kick was heading for the bottom right-hand corner of the net when Schmeichel flung himself down to push it away. United had got out of jail. What followed, however, was even more unbelievable.

In the second period of extra time, Arsenal's French midfielder, Patrick Vieira, misplaced a pass, and Ryan Giggs intercepted.

Going round Vieira, Giggs took off. He slipped round the outside of Lee Dixon. Then he shimmied in between the challenges of Dixon again and of Martin Keown, reminding everyone why he had been compared in the past to George Best.

By now Giggs had reached the edge of the Arsenal penalty area. Barely pausing to look up, he unleashed a rising drive which soared past Seaman. It was instantly hailed as one of the greatest goals ever seen – and it put United in the FA Cup Final.

It seemed inconceivable that such a performance could be matched. In fact, it was surpassed, seven days later in Turin. Only eleven minutes into the second leg of the Champions' League semi-final, Juventus were two goals up. Both came from Filippo Inzaghi, let in twice by slack defending. The Juventus supporters were already cheering victory. Their celebrations were premature.

In the twenty-fifth minute, Beckham crossed from the left. Suddenly, sailing above the Italian defenders was Roy Keane, who placed his header beyond the goalkeeper into the far corner of the net. United were reborn. Within nine minutes, Dwight Yorke appeared from nowhere in the Juventus penalty area with a diving header from a Cole cross, to make the scores level.

In the second half, the action was non-stop. Inzaghi had a goal disallowed, Irwin hit a post. Schmeichel, and in particular, Stam, were magnificent in United's defence. The Dutchman had grown in stature as the season had progressed, and he showed, more than ever on this night, why Ferguson had paid so much money for him.

With the score at 2–2, United were already ahead on the away goals rule. But they were not finished yet. Yorke rode two challenges with only six minutes left, before being brought down by goalkeeper Peruzzi. The referee played the advantage rule as the ball ran loose, and Cole tapped it in.

As Alex Ferguson is fond of saying, United had, as usual, made it hard for themselves. The bad news was that yellow cards for Keane and Paul Scholes meant that both would miss the final. But, for the first time since 1968, United were on the brink of winning the trophy they most coveted. They were also in the FA Cup Final, while in the Premiership everything depended upon the final Sunday of the season.

There was only one blemish on United's otherwise perfect horizon. In their last-but-one league game they had drawn 0–0 at Blackburn Rovers. By doing so they condemned their former assistant manager, Brian Kidd – who had left Old Trafford to become Blackburn's manager halfway through the season – to relegation and the First Division. Alex Ferguson was not even aware of the fate of his old friend and the mentor to so many of United's current team, until it was pointed out to him immediately after the match by a TV interviewer.

Three games in ten days would now decide whether or not United could achieve the greatest feat in English football history.

CHAPTER ELEVEN

16 MAY –
THE PREMIERSHIP
DECIDER

O n the final day of the season, two matches kicked off at the same time to decide the destiny of the 1998–9 FA Premiership. United, at home to Tottenham Hotspur, were a point ahead at the top. But they knew that they could not afford anything less than a win, as second-placed Arsenal were also at home, to Aston Villa.

Although Tottenham had nothing to play for except pride, the result was anything but a foregone conclusion. Under George Graham, whose record of managerial success in English football was second only to Alex Ferguson's, Spurs had recently been transformed from a team of under-achievers into one which had just won the Worthington Cup.

Arsenal fans feared that their north London bitter rivals would rather go through the motions and allow United to win than hand the Gunners the title. But their worries were unfounded. After a couple of early chances had gone begging, a long goal-kick by keeper Ian Walker was headed on by Steffen Iversen to Les Ferdinand in the twenty-fourth minute. Forcing himself ahead of Ronny Johnsen, Ferdinand then executed a delicate chip which went over Schmeichel and dropped into the net.

Spurs showed no sign of wishing to relinquish that lead easily either. Walker made a brilliant double save from Paul Scholes, full-back Stephen Carr blocked an attempt from Dwight Yorke, and both David Beckham and David May headed over the bar.

Watching in the stands were the assistant manager and chief scout of Bayern Munich, United's European Cup Final opponents. They had already been encouraged to note that Jaap Stam was missing through injury. Now they awaited with interest to see if United had the character to overcome their setback.

Their answer came in the forty-second minute. Scholes won a tussle with Tim Sherwood in midfield, played a one–two with Ryan Giggs, and then stroked a pass into the penalty area, after spotting Beckham making a forward run. His blazing shot was partially stopped by Walker, but the force of the strike carried the ball on, hitting a post before going in.

At half-time, Ferguson brought on Andy Cole for Teddy Sheringham. It was a decision which was repaid in one minute and forty-seven seconds. Running on to a pass from Gary Neville, Cole flighted the ball over Walker. The goal banished the unhappy memories Cole still harboured of the corresponding day of the 1994–5 season, when he had missed a succession of chances at West Ham, in a draw which had handed the Premiership to Blackburn Rovers.

Although Arsenal also managed to win, their 1–0 victory over Villa was in vain. Despite a nervous last forty minutes, United maintained their lead, prompted by fierce tackling from Keane, despite the ankle injury he was carrying.

The 'Theatre of Dreams', as Old Trafford was called, had lived up to its name, especially for Peter Schmeichel. It was his last game at the ground after eight years at the club, as he had previously announced that he would leave at the end of the season. He collected his fifth Premiership medal; for others, like Dwight Yorke and Teddy Sheringham, it was their first.

Alex Ferguson could not contain his pride. 'We deserved the title because we are the best team in the country. We have to take ourselves to the wire all the time, but we proved there is something about certain teams that elevates them beyond the rest. We just never give in.'

CHAPTER TWELVE

22 MAY –
THE FA CUP FINAL

Alex Ferguson had never looked so relaxed. As the sun beat down on the United players as they strolled around the Wembley pitch before returning to the dressing rooms to prepare for the FA Cup Final against Newcastle United, the manager chatted amiably to fans and signed autographs. Even in the tunnel, as the two teams lined up, there was a broad smile, and a word of encouragement for the team's young mascot.

If Newcastle took this apparent absence of tension to mean that perhaps the old master already had one eye on the forthcoming European Cup Final and was not utterly concentrated on what was about to happen that afternoon, then they were sadly mistaken. Winning the FA Cup nine years ago had saved

Ferguson's job, and two subsequent wins in the competition, in 1994 and 1996, had done nothing to dampen his enthusiasm. For one day at least, Bayern Munich were forgotten.

Injuries and suspensions forced Ferguson to shuffle his squad again for the match. Denis Irwin was banned after a previous sending-off and was replaced by Phil Neville. The manager decided to save Jaap Stam for the European Cup Final, feeling he had not fully recovered from an injury to his Achilles tendon. Nicky Butt was also rested for the big one, four days later, and Dwight Yorke stayed on the bench too, his place going to Ole Gunnar Solskjaer instead.

The first two names on the team sheet had been Roy Keane and Paul Scholes. For both it was their last match of the season, because of their suspensions from the European Cup Final. For Keane, the season was to end even more quickly than he thought. Eight minutes after the kick-off, Newcastle midfielder Gary Speed clattered into United's captain, and he was forced to limp off. It was a premature and sad conclusion to what had been such a pivotal contribution to United's chase for the Treble.

However, Keane's substitution also led directly to United taking the lead. His replacement was Teddy Sheringham. The England international had been annoyed the previous weekend when Ferguson took him off at half-time in the Premiership decider against Tottenham. He had a point to prove – and he did it very quickly.

Sheringham had been on the pitch less than two minutes when Paul Scholes picked him out with a defence-splitting pass. Running smoothly on to the through ball, Sheringham swept it past the goalkeeper. 1–0.

From that moment on, United dominated the proceedings. David Beckham, in particular, was flawless in his distribution and tackling, as he moved to take over Keane's central midfield role. It made him the obvious choice to deputize for Keane in the same position against Bayern.

The sending-off against Argentina was forgotten. Beckham ran the game, even though it was his fifty-eighth appearance in United's sixty-two fixtures so far that season – more than any other team-mate. Ferguson explained: 'The only one I have played throughout it all has been Beckham. But, then, I know his nature. I know he has the best stamina of any player at this club.'

A second goal seemed inevitable, and it duly came in the fifty-third minute. A poor clearance was seized by Solskjaer, and Sheringham was once more instrumental, coolly guiding Solskjaer's pass into the path of the charging Scholes, who drove the ball low and hard into the far corner of the net.

It emerged afterwards that Scholes had been doubtful of playing in the FA Cup Final until the morning of the match. He had been struck by a chest infection earlier in the week, and he spent the days leading up to the Final confined to his room so that he didn't spread the virus to his team-mates.

United should have had more goals. Yorke, who came on as a substitute after an hour, headed over an open goal, and a beautifully weighted chip from Sheringham bounced off the bar. Poor Newcastle, who had been defeated by the same scoreline in the FA Cup Final, twelve months before, by Arsenal, rarely looked like threatening United's superiority.

Such was the control that United exerted on the match, that Ferguson felt safe enough in bringing on Jaap Stam for the last thirteen minutes, to give him some match practice, and as a test to see that his injury had cleared up.

As a still-limping Roy Keane went up the royal steps to collect the FA Cup, there was general agreement that Sheringham had been the star of the match. Ever since he had signed for United from Tottenham, Sheringham had suffered taunts from opposing fans about the fact that he had joined at the start of a season in which United had won nothing.

As he followed Keane and his team-mates to collect his medal, Sheringham was greeted by a smiling United chairman, Martin Edwards, who leaned forward and, referring to the chants that the player had endured all season, said: 'Show us your medals now, Teddy.'

Ferguson also paid tribute to Sheringham's

performance. 'He was a different class. Following Eric Cantona in here was always going to be difficult, and there was always going to be criticism. But Teddy has been a great buy for me. He has good presence and he brings control and composure to our play.'

The victory meant that United had won their third League and Cup Double in six seasons. Sir Bobby Charlton exclaimed: 'A number of times this year I've thought: "Maybe this is the one which is beyond them." Yet they just keep on doing it.'

After this match, they now had to do it one more time. The season's astonishing comebacks – 2–0 down to Juventus in eleven minutes, 1–0 down to Liverpool in the FA Cup with three minutes to go, facing a last-minute penalty against Arsenal in the FA Cup semi-final, right up to going a goal behind in their last Premiership match against Tottenham – all boiled down to a final defining ninety minutes in Barcelona.

All those great United players down the years: Duncan Edwards, Bobby Charlton, Denis Law, George Best, Bryan Robson, Eric Cantona, not a single one of them had achieved what now lay within the grasp of this Manchester United team. Two down, one to go.

CHAPTER THIRTEEN

26 MAY –
'THEY ALWAYS
SCORE . . .'

On the eve of the European Cup Final, Lothar Matthäus had quoted Gary Lineker's famous description of football as a game in which twenty-two men run around a ball and then the Germans win. But nobody had told Manchester United that. Maybe it was the fact that the match fell on the ninetieth anniversary of the birth of Sir Matt Busby. Maybe it was the memory of Alex Ferguson's rousing half-time speech, in which he had told the players: 'The Cup will be only six feet away from you at the end of this night. If you lose, you can't even touch it. Do not come back in here without giving your all.'

Maybe it was the sight of Bayern's goalscorer, Mario Basler, waving to the German fans and from the touchline conducting their chanting, even though there were still twenty-five minutes of normal time remaining. Teddy Sheringham, waiting to come on as a substitute at the time, was incensed. 'I wasn't best pleased,' he said. 'The Germans were getting very flash and a bit cocky, and it was only 1–0.'

Or maybe it was simply the knowledge that they had come back from even tighter spots than this over the season. Whatever it was, Manchester United were not about to give up on the Treble yet. Even so, as the game moved into injury time, it seemed to even their most optimistic fans that United's dream was over.

Then at ninety minutes and seventeen seconds, David Beckham attacked down the left wing again. His cross was blocked by Stefan Effenberg for a corner. As Beckham prepared to take the corner, there was a note of desperation in ITV commentator Clive Tyldesley's voice. 'Can Manchester United score?' he asked. 'They always score . . .'

Bayern had six defenders crowded into their penalty area. Sheringham, Solskjaer, Yorke and Stam were there for United. They looked around to see that coming to join them was Peter Schmeichel, who had raced up from his own goal. On the touchline, Alex Ferguson turned to his assistant, Steve McClaren, and shook his head in disbelief.

At ninety minutes and twenty-nine seconds, Beckham's kick swung over the six-yard box. His corners had unsettled Bayern all evening, and so did this one. The imposing figures of Schmeichel and Stam next to each other also proved a major distraction, drawing three Bayern defenders towards them.

The ball dropped at Dwight Yorke's feet. He struggled to control the ball, and instead gave it away to opposing defender, Thorsten Fink. Surely now Fink would hack the ball away to safety. Instead he miskicked.

The ball went only as far as Ryan Giggs, standing in the D of the penalty area. He'd spotted Sheringham lurking inside the six-yard box and he stroked the ball through to him. At ninety minutes and thirty-five seconds, Sheringham, sideways on to the goal-line, swivelled and struck the ball. He didn't hit it cleanly, but that didn't matter. It was in.

Unbelievable. That was what all United's fans were saying, either to each other as they hugged and danced in the stands, or simply to themselves, over and over again, still not quite able to comprehend what they had just seen.

Nor could Lothar Matthäus. The TV cameras switched to his motionless figure in the Bayern dug-out, seconds after Sheringham's goal. He looked dumbfounded. Matthäus had been substituted eleven minutes from the end of normal time – and maybe that was Bayern's greatest mistake. Who knows how they might have benefited from his enormous experience in such high-pressure situations if he had stayed on?

Bayern kicked off again with the *Nou Camp* still in pandemonium. Ole Gunnar Solskjaer won the ball, and immediately ran deep into Bayern's half, but the tenacious Kuffour was right with him. The ball went out for another corner. After ninety-two minutes and fifteen seconds, Beckham again shaped to take the corner. Two seconds later, his kick was met by Sheringham, darting in between Effenberg and Thomas Linke, and, with a flick of his head, he glanced the ball across the Bayern goalmouth. As it dropped, Solskjaer, on the edge of the six-yard box, instinctively stuck out a foot. The ball shot into the roof of the net.

It was too much for those watching to take in. They'd still been celebrating Sheringham's equalizer and getting ready for extra time. Now this. For a brief instant, the linesmen's flags were checked on either side. But no, neither of them were up. It really was a goal.

Solskjaer ran to one side of the goal and slid to his knees, his arms outstretched. Dwight Yorke and Ronny Johnsen were right behind him and, in seconds, the Norwegian was submerged beneath a scrum of red shirts. At the other end of the pitch, Peter Schmeichel was performing cartwheels in his penalty area.

Bayern's players crumpled to the ground. Italian referee Pierluigi Collina actually had to pick some of them up to force them to play out the time that was left. The demoralized Germans had barely re-started when Signor Collina blew the final whistle.

The most amazing three minutes of injury time ever witnessed was over. So, after thirty-one years, was Manchester United's quest for the European Cup. And, even in the moment of his greatest glory, it was the predecessor whose record he had now equalled whom Alex Ferguson remembered. 'It was so fitting that this day would have been the ninetieth birthday of Sir Matt. He will have been looking down on us and I think he'll have been doing a lot of kicking up there.'

The manager admitted that at the end of ninety minutes he was resigned to defeat. 'Before Teddy scored, I was starting to adjust my mind to losing the game. I was reminding myself to keep my dignity and to accept that this was not going to be our year after all.'

David Beckham dedicated the triumph to Ferguson. 'This is for him,' he said. 'He deserves everything he gets. He brought me up and has made my career what it is. So we all owe the manager everything.'

Two more incidents amid the joyful scenes in the *Nou Camp* Stadium illustrate the spirit of Manchester United. The first was when Peter Schmeichel, in his last appearance for United, went up to collect the two-foot-high silver trophy. Instead of immediately hoisting it aloft, he waited until the entire team, and Ferguson, were around him, before all of them lifted it together.

Then, as United posed for yet another victory photograph with the European Cup, Ferguson – who within three weeks would be knighted for his achievements and so share something else in common with Sir Matt Busby – spotted Roy Keane. Walking over, the manager took him by the arm and led him to join the rest of the wildly celebrating players.

For above all, the victory – and the Treble it completed – was a team effort, by a team that never knows when it is beaten. That much the UEFA official, who had hastily changed the ribbons on the handles of the European Cup just before the final whistle, now knew. This time there was no mistake. They were in the red and white of Manchester United.